W9-BFE-924

SuperSmart Systems

5 Simple, No-Nonsense Steps To Superiority In Reading Speed, Writing, Math, & Memory

Dr. Edward F. Droge, Jr.

Crimson Blue Publishing
Greenwich, NY 12834

for MARY and ABIGAIL

SuperSmart Systems. Copyright © 1994 by Edward F. Droge, Jr.

Printed and bound in the United States of America. All rights reserved. No portion of this book may be reproduced in any form, electronic or otherwise, including photocopying, faxing, and information storage and retrieval systems, without permission in writing from the copyright owner, Edward F. Droge, Jr., except by a reviewer, who may quote brief passages in a review.

This book is meant to enrich the reader's skills, and is not meant to substitute for sound educational pursuits in school, college, or elsewhere. The author and publisher assume no responsibility for any dissatisfaction with the methods put forth in this book, or the results realized by the reader, beyond a refund of the cost of the book within 30 days of purchase, upon return of the book in good, saleable condition. Shipping and handling costs of any returns are solely the responsibility of the person seeking the refund.

Published by Crimson Blue, Inc., P.O. Box 205, Greenwich, NY 12834. (518) 692-9000

First Printing 1994
00 99 98 97 96 95 94   10 9 8 7 6 5 4 3 2 1

ISBN 0-9637771-1-4 Hardback
ISBN 0-9637771-0-6 Paperback

CONTENTS

INTRODUCTION

Congratulations. By choosing to engage a program that will show you how to bring yourself to superior levels in four very important intellectual areas, you are separating yourself from the pack and joining a very special and select circle of SuperSmart people.

The concept behind SuperSmart Systems is simple: to present to the reader a clear, uncluttered method for learning how to reach superior levels in each area -- reading speed, writing, math, and memory. The program does not dwell on history or theory, but prefers to be practical by providing the methods directly for immediate implementation. Any history or theory necessary to facilitate the process is provided without undue elaboration.

With more than 20 years of experience in the world of Education, the author knows very well the importance of laying out each step in an easy-to-read, easy-to-grasp style, permitting the reader to gain command of the System quickly. As in any pursuit, however, practice is not only recommended but required to perfect the skills learned.

Just think of what it could mean to you if you were able to double or triple your reading speed. That is not an unreasonable goal in the reading speed section. Imagine, also, the rewards that lay ahead when you raise the level of your abilities in writing, math, and memory. Let the thought of those rewards motivate you to learn each System well.

Get ready. You are about to begin a fascinating journey that will bring you to a special place: you are about to learn how to become SuperSmart.

"Think without boundaries and expect much of yourself."

Dr. Edward F. Droge, Jr.

5 SIMPLE STEPS TO FASTER READING AND BETTER COMPREHENSION

by Dr. Edward F. Droge, Jr.

Have you ever measured your reading speed? How fast or slow are you? How many words per minute do you read? Whatever your speed, the chances are very good that you can improve by following the five simple steps outlined in this section.

PRESENT READING SPEED

First, let's check your reading speed in terms of a words-per-minute rate. Read the following passage at your **normal** reading speed. Do not concern yourself with how fast or slow others read or how fast or slow others think you read. Do not race through the passage. The object here is to measure your normal reading speed now so that we may get an accurate measurement of your improvement later.

This is not a contest: you are not competing with anyone to see who reads the fastest. If you are in a classroom or other area with people reading the same passage, do not concern yourself with the others around you: some may finish before you do. So what? Some people swim faster than others, some run faster, some read faster. Without question, many people read slower than you also. Your reading speed is a private matter that you may share only if you wish to share it.

It is important to measure your reading time exactly. Have a pen handy. When you are ready to begin reading, check the seconds of your watch or clock and jot down the **exact** time you begin. You must note the minutes AND seconds. Using the chart provided after the passage, you will convert your reading time into a words-per-minute rate.

Ready?

Record the exact current time in this space:
minute_____seconds_____.

Please read the passage now at your **normal** rate.

Faster Reading and Better Comprehension

Huck Finn is quite perceptive and uses his perception to the utmost in order to survive in the rough and tough, Southern river country in which he lives. With very little formal education, Huck relies on his senses to carry him through an adventurous life, filled with rafts and riverboats, exaggerations and lies, river-islands and hideouts, strange towns and strange people, con games and con artists, injured men and dead bodies, friendship and slavery, storms and rattlesnakes, Tom Sawyer and The Royal Nonesuch, and more. Huck compensates for a lack of classroom training and information by accumulating an abundance of people-contact and life-experience: his senses are his books, the river his classroom, the many people he meets his teachers. Without his keen senses, he would not be able to survive as admirably as he does. Twain permeates the book with instances when Huck "sees" and "hears" and "feels." Huck's senses are the means by which he gains knowledge, and he uses them often and well. He enjoys using his senses, and, when possible, he lies back to absorb all that he can see or hear. Easily enough, his perception enables him to provide detailed descriptions to "read" the river, to tell time without a watch, to discern revealing characteristics of a footprint, to recognize acquaintances through an ugly mask of tar and feathers, and to judge a person's character or personality with amazing accuracy. Huck is always ready to employ his senses, and relies on them to keep him safe. When his senses are impaired, trouble threatens and he is apt to suffer. When one sense is useless, he switches to another: if he cannot see, he feels or listens, to guard himself from potential harm.

The reader is constantly informed of what Huck sees or does not see, what he hears or cannot hear, what he touches, what he tastes, what he smells. Threatened with being caught holding a bag of money he has taken from the king and duke, Huck shoves it into a coffin and accidentally touches the corpse's hands, which makes him creepy because they're so cold. Sitting down to dinner with Tom Sawyer and his aunt, Huck is pleasantly surprised at the meal in front of him: there was enough food, he says, to feed seven families -- and he is impressed that it's all hot and that the meat is not tough, the kind that lies in the cellar for nights at a time, the kind that tastes strange in the morning. Observing the audience of a third-night performance by The Royal Nonesuch, Huck notices that every man has bulging pockets and he smells foul things, like rotten eggs and cabbage, and maybe even dead cats -- sixty-four dead cats, he guesses.

Examples such as these of Huck's touching, tasting and smelling can be culled from nearly every chapter. Alone, each may seem insignificant to Huck's character, but collectively they form the core of his existence. And Huck is aware of this. More than once he lets us know the importance of his perception. For example, his perception informs him that people are influenced by the way a person is dressed; his perception enables him to judge the gravity of a situation or seriousness of a person; his perception tells him that there are many ways to view the same thing, that is, interpretations may vary according to the perspective taken. To illustrate, Huck notices the influence of a man's dress when the king changes into his store-bought clothes: Huck says he never realized

how clothes could change a person: while earlier, with
his old clothes, the king looked like an ornery old
timer, now, with his new hat and tie and smile, he
looked so different, so noticeably different, like
Leviticus, he says. As for the gravity of a situation,
many times Huck is able to sense trouble simply by a
person's expression. The duke and king serve as
examples when Huck says of them at one point that he
can see trouble in their look. And at another point
when he is talking with Mary Jane he notes her
expression and determines without question that she is
dead serious: he notes her spreading nostrils and her
snapping eyes. But Huck also knows that he must be
flexible: things are not always as simple as they at first
may seem. A lot depends on <u>how</u> you look, that is, on
what perspective you take. For example, Huck sees
watermelon being brought to the hut, but figures it is
for the dogs. When Tom tells him that the watermelon
is more likely for Jim, Huck agrees and thinks about it
for a moment. It never occurred to him, he says, that a
dog might not eat watermelon. Funny, he thinks, how
a person can see something but not really see it for
what it is.

     That Huck's senses are keen is evinced by,
among other things, his very detailed descriptions, his
ability to read the river and footprints, and his ability to
discern even in the most trying circumstances. When
Huck describes a person or place, the reader is given a
very detailed account. Of the Grangerford home, for
example, he tells us that it has brass doorknobs, a big,
clean, bricked fireplace with brass dog-irons, a clock
with an intricate picture painted on it -- an intimate
account of which he gives us, from top to middle to

bottom, including a description of the swinging pendulum -- a gaudy chalk parrot on each side of the clock, a crockery dog and cat that squeaked when you pressed them but did not do anything else that made them remarkable in any way, a couple of fans made of wild turkey wings, and on and on and on. Of Colonel Grangerford himself, Huck reports that he is tall, very slim, clean-shaven, thin-lipped, with a high nose, thin nostrils, heavy eyebrows, high forehead, blackish eyes, straight black hair that hung to his shoulders, long, thin hands, and so on. The point is, of course, that not very much escapes Huck's perception of people or places, not very much at all.

———————
———————

CHECK YOUR CLOCK OR WATCH AND RECORD THE EXACT CURRENT TIME HERE minute_____seconds_____.

Determine the number of minutes and seconds it took to read the passage. (Subtract start from finish.)

RECORD YOUR TOTAL READING TIME: ____minutes _____seconds

Now check the conversion chart on the next page to determine your words-per-minute rate.

CONVERSION CHART (Find the time closest to your Total Reading Time.)

minutes/seconds = words-per-minute

9min/50secs =102; 9/40 = 103; 9/30 = 105; 9/20 = 107
9/10 = 109; 9/00 = 111;

8/50 = 113; 8/40 = 115; 8/30 = 118; 8/20 = 120;
8/10 = 123; 8/00 = 125

7/50 = 128; 7/40 = 130; 7/30 = 133; 7/20 = 136;
7/10 = 140; 7/00 = 143

6/50 = 146; 6/40 = 150; 6/30 = 154; 6/20 = 158;
6/10 = 162; 6/00 = 167

5/50 = 171; 5/40 = 176; 5/30 = 182; 5/20 = 188;
5/10 = 194; 5/00 = 200

4/50 = 207; 4/40 = 214; 4/30 = 222; 4/20 = 231;
4/10 = 240; 4/00 = 250

3/50 = 261; 3/40 = 273; 3/30 = 286; 3/20 = 300;
3/10 = 316; 3/00 = 333

2/50 = 353; 2/40 = 375; 2/30 = 400; 2/20 = 429;
2/10 = 462; 2/00 = 500

1/50 = 545; 1/40 = 600; 1/30 = 667; 1/20 = 750;
1/10 = 857; 1/00 = 1000

RECORD YOUR WPM RATE HERE_____.

This might be the first time you have ever measured your reading speed, but it should not be the last. Following the five simple steps below will improve your rate, perhaps dramatically. **You can improve your reading if you try.**

For most people, reading occupies hours and hours each week: students read for school, sunbathers read leisurely on the beach, commuters read on the subway or the bus. Whether it's a novel, a magazine, the daily newspaper, or a business report, there always seems to be something nearby that beckons to be read. No one would disagree that reading plays an important role in our lives -- as a medium for business, for pleasure, for education -- with occupations and lifestyles determining the different demands.

For many, however, reading takes up much more time than it should. Some people, in fact, view the act of reading as a chore, intimidating, anything but enjoyable: "The book looks too thick." "The subject matter is unattractive." "I have to read it, but I don't want to read it."

Whether you like to read or not, and whether you are intimidated by a thick book or attracted to it, you ought to know that you can read faster if you try. In fact, **doubling your reading speed is not an unreasonable goal**. Think of what doubling your reading speed could mean to you: the book that now takes you four hours to read would take you only two; you could read two books in the time it now takes you to read one!

But the purpose of this system is not to increase your reading speed to a phenomenal 2000 words-per-minute rate. Rather, the purpose is to present a simple (i.e. not complicated) way for you to read faster than you presently do. Personal improvement and reasonable goals are encouraged. You must remember always that faster reading can be achieved only with practice. There is no easy way to better reading skills. There is, however, a simple way, a path that is not cluttered with complex obstacles.

PACE YOURSELF

Be aware that "speed" reading is just not practical at times. Technical material may be difficult to negotiate. A science textbook, for example, is not ideal for speed reading practice. That is not to say, however, that the method put forth in this system cannot be used with technical material; rather, the speed which you choose should depend on the difficulty of the material you are reading, in the same way that the use of low gear and high gear on a bicycle or car depends on whether the vehicle is going up the hill or down.

Of course, you may choose to read leisurely at any time. Reading should be fun, and reading at your own pace is always an option. But certainly you should have the option to read quickly if you want to, or need to, and once you learn -- like learning to ride a bicycle -- you'll never forget.

STEP # 1. PREVIEW THE READING

Before you begin to read at length, get a general idea of the content of what is to be read. This will permit you to understand the subject matter a bit more when actually reading, and also will help you to be more receptive to the material.

If, for example, you are about to read an article or report, begin by reading the first and last sentence of each paragraph. If this is not practical for some reason (maybe the article or report is very long, and you do not have much time), at least read the first sentence of each paragraph. Generally, the first sentence of each paragraph is loaded with information about what is to follow. By reading the first sentence, you will acquire a general knowledge of the piece. **This will improve your comprehension** when you read the entire piece, since you will be prepared a bit for what the writer wants to tell you.

KEY WORDS AND PHRASES

Skim the article for key words and phrases like: **most important; in conclusion; in summary; never; always;** etc. If you read a paragraph that begins "In summary," you will, of course, have a very good idea about the content of the piece. **This will improve your comprehension.**

In addition, skim the article for words, phrases, and sentences that are **underlined** or in **quotation**

marks or bold print. <u>**This will improve your**</u> <u>**comprehension.**</u> The writer often uses underlining or bold print for emphasis, or to draw your attention to something that is important. Quotations are worth noting, and may reveal memorable opinions.

SURVEY

If you are about to read a book, first **survey** the title page, the copyright date, the contents page, the dust jacket, the preface, and whatever else might give you a general idea of what the author wants you to know. <u>**This will improve your comprehension.**</u> You can find out a lot about a book even before you read it.

Can you think of other ways to preview the reading? If so, do not hesitate to use them. Don't underestimate the importance of previewing; it will make you a better reader.

IN SUMMARY (Step #1)

Preview the reading by:

--reading the first sentence of each paragraph
--skimming the piece for key words and phrases
--looking for quotation marks,underlines, bold print
--surveying a book
--using other methods of your own.

STEP # 2. SEE MORE

You are capable of seeing more than you presently see when you read. The eye is an amazing instrument, and all too often we underuse it.

When you first learned how to read, your teacher marked your progress by listening to you "read aloud." But when you do read aloud, you can <u>say</u> only one word at a time and, therefore, you <u>look at</u> only one word at a time. **Your reading speed is slowed up considerably by seeing only one word at a time.**

TRY THIS

Hold up two fingers. Look at the finger on the right. While looking at the finger on the right, you can still see the finger on the left. Move the finger on the left. You saw it move, didn't you?

When you look at a car driving by, you see the whole car, don't you? When you are at the zoo, looking at an elephant, you see the whole elephant, don't you? Of course you can see more than one little word at a time. You simply need to retrain yourself to do so. Now look at the following pairs of words:

> the book
> good luck
> my tie
> thanks, pal
> main event

Look at the word on the right. When you look at "book," you notice that there is another word to the left, though you may not be able to see clearly that it is the word "the." The same is true with each pair: when looking at the word on the right, you can see that there is a word to the left, though you may not be able to see it clearly.

Now **draw back your focus** when you look at each pair of words. Instead of looking directly at the word on the right, look **between** the two words. Focus your eyes so that you can see and **understand** both words. This may take some practice at first. Keep trying until you master it.

Your focus does not have to be exactly between the two words. Where you have to focus in order to see both words clearly may be different from where someone else has to focus. Your personal focal point, the one that is comfortable for **you**, is what you should look for now.

You can do it, no matter how old you are or how long you have been underusing your eyes. It may take some people a little bit more practice than others, but you know you can do it -- remember that you saw **both** of your fingers before. Now you must see more on the written page.

Practice looking at the above pairs of words and any other pairs of words until you can see clearly **both** words at the same time. **When you can see more, your reading speed will improve.**

HOW MANY STOPS?

If there are 12 words on a line and you focus on only one word at a time, your eyes will stop 12 times on that line. **Unnecessary "eye stops" waste precious time.**

You have been instructed to see two words at a time, just as you saw both your fingers and both words in the given pairs. Now if there are 12 words on a line and you see 2 at a time, your eyes will stop only 6 times on that line. In effect, you have the tools necessary to double your reading speed already, since, with practice, it will take you only half the amount of time it did previously to read that line.

Take the "refocusing" method and develop the theory one step further: see 3 words at a time. A line with 12 words would require only 4 stops. **Theoretically, if you master this, you will have tripled your reading speed!**

IT'S UP TO YOU

Do you want to read faster? This "refocus" is not a very difficult process, but it takes practice. Don't forget, you have been reading as you now read for many, many years. **You must retrain yourself to break an old habit. But you can do it.** And always remind yourself of what awaits you when you succeed. Just imagine what it would be like if you doubled or tripled your reading speed. And no one says you must stop there.

AN IMPORTANT NOTE

Your goal now should be to master the technique of refocusing to see more, and it would not be unusual at first if you had to read slower than you presently read in order to accomplish this goal. Don't worry; the speed will come. But you must master the technique at a speed that is comfortable. You must not expect to be able to double or triple your reading speed without practice. Once you have mastered the technique, you will have opened the door to the rewards of faster reading and better comprehension. But, for now, read only as fast (or as slow) as you have to, in order to feel that you **see more.**

VERY, VERY IMPORTANT -- BE PRACTICAL

You must keep something in mind as you practice this "refocus." It is better if you train yourself right from the start to see phrases or blocks of words, rather than merely seeing every 2 or 3 words. Be practical whenever you can.

For example, suppose you are practicing, and you want to see 2 words at a time, and you come to a line that contains the following: "...Jack sat in the chair..."

Seeing "Jack sat" in one stop of the eyes certainly would be fine. But, if in the next stop you saw only "in the," then you might be making the process more difficult than it should be.

Try to see the whole phrase, "in the chair." Your mind will accept the whole phrase quite readily. By seeing phrases or commonly related blocks of words, rather than strictly 2 words per stop, you will save yourself an unnecessary and awkward step.

In the beginning, you may have difficulty understanding what you are reading while you are retraining your eyes -- **this is to be expected and will be temporary only**. Once you master the skill, you can expect better comprehension.

Give yourself all the advantages and opportunities that you can. If you can understand "of the house" more easily than "of the" and "house...," then you should see or focus on the whole phrase "of the house." **See phrases or blocks of words whenever practical.**

EXERCISE

Find a long article in a magazine or newspaper, or turn to any page of a novel. **With the intention of seeing 2 or 3 words at a time**, take a pencil and circle the word, words, phrases, or blocks of words that you can see at each eye stop. Don't worry at all about comprehension for this exercise.

Read slowly while practicing your new method of focusing. Be honest with yourself when circling the words. **Do not read on in this section until you have finished this exercise.**

IF YOU HAVE COMPLETED THE EXERCISE, PLEASE CONTINUE...

YOU CAN DO IT

You should not be surprised if your circles got bigger and bigger as you went along. You saw more and more as you progressed. Your eyes are already responding to the task. They are quite capable of "seeing more" than you have asked them to see in the past. Your retraining has begun. And you should not be surprised if your comprehension was low with this exercise. Good comprehension comes when you master the technique.

If your circles did not get bigger, and if you did not see more as you progressed, do not despair. All this means for you is a little more practice. It will come. Be encouraged. Think "positive." Do not be discouraged if you do not master immediately any suggestions in this system. It is not easy to be good at anything. Be confident that with practice your reading will improve and that you will reap the benefits that go along with it. Every successful person knows that the key to success is: "Don't give up."

IN SUMMARY (Step #2)

See more:

--refocus to see more than one word per stop
--retrain yourself to break an old habit
--master the technique, even if you must read slower to do so -- it is only temporary
--be practical: see phrases or blocks of words
--don't worry about low comprehension now; good comprehension comes when you master the technique
--be confident that you can do it
--practice, practice, practice.

ASSIGNMENT

Read as much as you can. Practice seeing more than one word per stop. Master Step #2 before moving to Step #3.

FORMULA FOR MEASURING

If you wish to monitor your progress by measuring your reading speed regularly, here is a simple formula that will help: To measure your words-per-minute rate, you will need to know how many words you have read in the passage, and exactly how many seconds it took to read. Once you know these figures, calculate your words-per-minute rate as follows: **(Total Words in Passage x 60) divided by (Number of Seconds) = Words-per-minute.**

(You can estimate the number of words in a passage by determining the average number of words per line and by multiplying that by the number of lines. Of course, if the text is laid out unevenly, the average number of words per line may be difficult to determine.)

If you estimate the number of words in a passage or the time it took to read, the words-per-minute rate is not very reliable. Estimating is fine occasionally, but try to be as exact as you can as often as you can.

STEP # 3. 3 STOPS PER LINE

Congratulations! Since you now see more than one word per eye stop, your reading speed has improved. You are now ready to advance even further.

The next step is a logical advance. Since you have retrained yourself to see more than one word each time you focus within a line of print, you must put that skill to work by forcing yourself to make **a maximum of 3 stops per line.**

EXERCISE

Below you will see a series of blocks of x's, three blocks per line. As you look at each line, **focus on each whole block only as long as it takes you to see it all clearly**, then move your eyes to the next block, focus, then move to the third and last block on the line and focus. After a clear focus on the third block, move your eyes to the beginning of the next line and focus on its first block. Repeat the process.

This exercise is designed to train your eyes to make **only 3 distinct stops per line**. Now, of course, you will be focusing on blocks of x's, but soon you will substitute words. Your eyes must get used to, and be comfortable with, 3 stops per line. **Practice until you feel you have mastered the skill.**

xxxxxxxxxx   xxxxxxxxxx   xxxxxxxxxx

xxxxxxxxxx   xxxxxxxxxx   xxxxxxxxxx

xxxxxxxxxx   xxxxxxxxxx   xxxxxxxxxx

xxxxxxxxxx   xxxxxxxxxx   xxxxxxxxxx

xxxxxxxxxx   xxxxxxxxxx   xxxxxxxxxx

GRADUATION

You are ready to graduate from blocks of x's to words. In the same way that you trained your eyes to make only 3 stops per line with the blocks, focusing on each whole block with each stop, now you will train your eyes to make only 3 stops per line with printed words.

NOTE WELL

When you begin to practice, you will notice that different magazines, newspapers, books, and other reading materials have lines of print that vary in size and length. Even within the same magazine or newspaper, the lines vary in length.

For example, in the New York Times on any Sunday, there are several sections. In the "news" section, each column of print may have only 6 or 7 words per line. But in "The Book Review," each column of print may have as many as 15 words per line. **You can use varying lengths of printed lines to your benefit.**

STRATEGY

Since you are going to make only 3 stops per line, each stop or focus should take-in approximately 1/3 of the line (allowing, of course, for being practical - - that is, if a phrase or group of commonly related words, like "in the house," cause you to take in more than 1/3, this is perfectly acceptable; in fact, it is encouraged).

The best path for you in your training is a **gradual progression**. Therefore, read the shorter length lines in the beginning, and work your way up to the longer lengths. For example, if a column of newsprint has about 6 words per line, and you are to make 3 stops per line, then with each stop you should take in, or focus on, 2 words (1/3 of the line). If there are 15 words in the line, you will be asking your eyes to take in 5 words with each stop. It would be best for you to make a gradual progression, from 2 words per stop to 5 words per stop.

Begin practicing with narrow columns of newspapers or magazines, making only 3 stops per line. When you feel you are ready to advance, practice with reading materials that contain more words per line. You are not encouraged to begin with books, since usually there are too many words per line.

HELPFUL HINT

You may find it easier in the beginning to guide yourself into making only 3 stops per line by putting 3 pencil dots (placed in line with where you intend to make your eye stops)   on the very top and very bottom of what you intend to read. You may want to think of an **imaginary line** connecting the dots, if it makes it easier for you to stop in about the same spot on each line. (See illustration A)

Illustration A

.   .   .

Huck's senses are the means by which he
gains knowledge, and he uses them often
and well. He enjoys using his senses, and,
when possible, he lies back to absorb all
that he can see or hear. Easily enough,
his perception enables him to provide
detailed descriptions, to "read" the river,
and to tell time without a watch.

.   .   .

GUIDE YOURSELF

In the beginning it might also help if you used a pen or pencil, or even your finger, to guide you in your 3 stops. On each line, make 3 distinct stops with your pen, pencil, or finger, following along with your focus, spacing the stops so that your eyes can take in 1/3 of the line.

You may even wish to use the dots <u>and</u> your finger to guide yourself. Line up your finger stops with the dots. Whatever method you use, it is acceptable as long as it strives to make you feel comfortable while it helps you to master the skill quickly and easily.

If, while you are practicing, you come to lines that need only 2 stops, you are encouraged to make only 2 stops. Perhaps, for example, you come to a line with only 2 lengthy words taking up the whole line. Three stops in this case would be counterproductive, especially if you can take in each whole word with one eye stop. So, if you can read a line with only 2 stops, don't fight it; do it.

Find something to read and practice this technique of 3 stops per line. Pace your speed to maintain comprehension, but know that both high speed and high comprehension will come with practice. **The more you practice, the quicker you will master the skill.**

IN SUMMARY (Step #3)

Make only 3 stops per line:

--practice with the blocks of x's until your eyes get used to 3 distinct stops
--when you are ready to practice with words, make a gradual progression; in the beginning, the fewer words per line, the better

--remember always to be practical, taking in phrases and groups of commonly related words whenever possible
--use dots and/or your finger to guide you
--low comprehension and slow reading in the beginning are to be expected; do not be discouraged
--the more you practice, the quicker you will master the skill.

ASSIGNMENT

Your assignment is to read as much as you can before moving on. Practice making only 3 stops per line. Follow the guidelines for a gradual progression.

STEP # 4. 2 STOPS PER LINE

Congratulations are in order again. You are well on your way to the goal you have set for yourself. And the next step follows naturally.

Instead of 3 stops per line, now you will make only 2 stops per line. The theory is the same: take in more with each focus. Now, however, you will train your eyes to take in 1/2 of the line with each eye stop.

GRADUAL PROGRESSION AGAIN

As with the 3 stops per line, you should aim for a gradual progression with 2 stops per line. First, get comfortable with 2 stops. Use the blocks of x's below in the same way that you used them before: practice focusing, moving on, focusing, etc.

Again, you should use varying lengths of printed lines to your benefit. Start with narrow columns in newspapers and magazines, and work your way up to books.

Below, see each **whole** block of x's before moving on.

        xxxxxxxxxx   xxxxxxxxxx

        xxxxxxxxxx   xxxxxxxxxx

        xxxxxxxxxx   xxxxxxxxxx

HINTS

When you move from the blocks of x's to actual reading, don't forget to be practical--take in phrases and groups of commonly related words whenever possible. Use the dots again, except now only 2 dots, making sure they are properly spaced. And use your finger, or pen, or pencil to guide yourself, if it helps. Low speed and comprehension may be expected in the beginning.

You need not worry that each stop takes in exactly one-half of the line. You need to keep in mind only that you are to make a maximum of 2 stops per line. One-half of the line per stop is merely a guide.

IN SUMMARY (Step #4)

Make only 2 stops per line:

--practice with the blocks of x's until your eyes get used to 2 distinct stops
--when you are ready to practice with words, make a natural progression -- narrow newspaper columns to books
--always be practical, seeing whole phrases when possible
--use dots and your finger to guide you
--low speed and comprehension may be expected in the beginning; do not be discouraged
--practice, practice, practice.

ASSIGNMENT

Read as much as you can -- as much as it takes -- to master the skill.

MEASURE YOUR PRESENT READING SPEED

Let's find out how fast you read now. If you have mastered the skills, you should be able to see much more with each eye stop.

The last step -- Step #5 -- concerns comprehension, so, for now, do not be too concerned with how well you comprehend. But, at the same time, **do not be surprised if you feel your comprehension is improving**, even if you are making no conscious effort to understand or retain more. You will learn why this happens in Step #5.

For now, just be concerned with your present reading speed. Have a pen handy. Check your watch or clock and read the following passage.

Record the current time: ____minutes ____seconds

The keenness of Huck's senses permits him to interpret the river as a person who lives on it must. Often he maneuvers up and down and across the river, paddling or floating from shore to shore, sojourning on river-islands of tangled wood, avoiding debris and sand bars, ever on the lookout for riverboats, the shore line, the signs of land. No city boy could perceive the river the way Huck does. One particular time, for example, he tells us about seeing a streak in the water, which, he knows, signifies that there is a certain snag in the current which makes the streak look that certain way. He knows, therefore, how swift the current is.

Huck's keenness of perception is also exhibited by his discerning eye. When he sees footprints in the snow outside his aunt's house, he is curious, and upon closer examination he notes that there is a certain cross in one of the heels made by two nails of the boot. He knows immediately that it is his father's footprint. More dramatically, he sees a riotous gang carrying two tarred and feathered people out of town on a rail, and knows immediately who they are: he knew it was the king and duke, he says, even though they had tar and feathers from head to toe, making them look hardly human, let alone recognizable. He just knew.

Adding to the effectiveness of his perception, Huck is always on guard with his senses. At one point in the beginning of the book, Huck escapes his father and rushes through the woods. Repeatedly he tells us how he listens and watches, listens and watches: his strategy is to stay in the thick of the woods where the ground is deeply covered with leaves, and every once in a while he stops to listen and look. Surely he will hear or see anyone in the vicinity. At another point the reader cannot help thinking that Twain is overtly emphasizing Huck's reliance on perception. Jim and Huck are camped on an island, passing the time with conversation, when Huck interrupts, asking the others if they hear a noise. They investigate and find that it was only the paddle of a far off steamboat, so they relax and resume their conversation. There is little or no reason for this interruption other than the author's wish to stress the importance or quality of Huck's perception. That Huck does rely on his perception to keep him safe is obvious.

But Huck does not use his senses only to guard against danger; rather, he uses them whenever he can. He enjoys lying down and sucking in everything his senses will record. On one occasion he tells us that he grew a bit lonely and so he went to the bank of the river so that he could simply listen to the water as it rushes by and so that he could count the stars and the driftwood and the rafts as they pass. There is no better way, he tells, to counteract the feeling you get when you are lonely. On another occasion he tells us about how he is inclined to lie down in his canoe and let it float among the driftwood on the river, resting, smoking his pipe, scanning the sky and noting that nary a cloud was to be seen. He marvels at how vast the sky is and how far a person can see at night on the water in the light of the moon. And on yet another occasion Huck reports that, even though it is dark at night on the river, a spark from a passing raft, or a fiddler's song, would alert you to the traffic passing by. What could be better, he wonders, than to lie on your back on a raft, watching the stars and listening to the river all around you? Twain gives us a character who has keen perception, who uses it, and who enjoys it.

But often Huck's senses are impaired, and when this happens he must be ever careful of impending trouble. A constant nemesis on the river is fog, and the fogs Huck encounters are thick and difficult to negotiate: he penetrates a fog once, he tells us, and he loses all idea of direction. Without sight to help him,

he switches to hearing. He and Jim have become
separated in the fog and Huck decides to yell, hoping
Jim will answer. His spirits are buoyed when he hears
a faint yell in response. He heads toward it, all the
time listening, listening, listening. But he soon
discovers that his hopes of locating Jim had been
premature: when he hears the faint yell again, it is
behind him this time and each time it comes it seems to
be coming from a different place. He is frustrated and
he acknowledges just how confusing a fog can be.
Nothing looks or sounds normal in a fog, he says. He
echoes the same thoughts when caught in another fog
later in the book. A scow or raft passes Huck's raft so
closely that voices could be heard, though people could
not be seen: he tells us that he can hear them clearly
though he cannot see them at all; it spooks him and
makes him think of ghostly things. But Huck knows
that his senses will get him through the fog eventually,
and he never gives up. He knows that as long as he
can sit still, keep quiet and listen, he will be fine. More
than this, though, he knows that even if his vision or
hearing are impaired by the fog, his sixth sense will pull
him through, his sense of "feeling". This is not to be
confused with the sense of touching. Feeling is best
described as a judgment based on intuition. Huck has
feelings throughout the novel, and is alert enough to
know that sometimes they may be deceptive. Lost in a
fog once, he is aware that he is floating along at four or
five miles an hour, even though, he says, you feel as if
you are not moving at all in the water.

CHECK YOUR CLOCK OR WATCH AND
RECORD THE CURRENT TIME HERE
minutes_____seconds_____.

Determine the number of minutes and seconds it took
to read the passage. (Subtract start from finish.)

RECORD YOUR TOTAL READING TIME:
_____minutes _____seconds.

Now check the Conversion Chart on page 7 to
determine your words-per-minute rate.

RECORD YOUR NEW WPM RATE HERE
_____.

COMPARE

Compare your present words-per-minute rate
with the rate you were reading when you started this
system (See bottom of page 7). You should see an
improvement. Congratulations. If you would like to
improve even more, you must practice more.

Now that your speed is improving, turn to Step
#5 for concentration on better comprehension.

STEP # 5. BETTER COMPREHENSION

Do you ever get to the end of a paragraph and realize that you don't know what you just read? The reason: your mind wanders. Perhaps you were thinking of the good-looking male or female next door, or the test you will take tomorrow, or all the work you have to do -- so many things can crowd your mind and force you to lose your concentration.

WHAT YOU CAN DO

Reading at the proper speed will combat mind-wandering. The principle is very simple: if you are concentrating on the proper speed, you will not be able to concentrate on anything else. Your mind will not be permitted to wander.

What is the proper speed for you? **Only you know.** Not too fast, not too slow -- each person's proper speed is a personal decision. You must feel comfortable with your reading. You will not feel optimum comfort if you read at a speed that someone else chooses for you.

A MYTH

Many people believe that the slower one reads, the better one comprehends. No research supports this myth. As a matter of fact, just the opposite has been proven to be true -- the slower one reads, the less one comprehends. The reason: the mind is permitted to wander. One thing is certain: good comprehension is recorded when one reads at a **proper** speed, not a slow speed. Again, proper speed varies from individual to individual.

Find your proper speed and concentrate on it while you are reading. Do not permit your mind to wander.

OTHER CONSIDERATIONS

Give yourself a chance for good comprehension. Even if you think that the television or stereo is not bothering you while you are reading, you are not giving your mind the isolation it deserves when attempting to concentrate on reading matter. If it is loud enough to hear, a television or stereo, even in the next room, can be harmful to your reading. You can't close out the world, but you can try to create optimum conditions.

Find a quiet place to read. Close the door, if possible. Be sure the lighting is good, and don't get too comfortable in your chair unless you seek to go to sleep.

CHECKS IN THE MARGINS

As you read, put checks in the margins when you get to a part that you think is important. Checks in the margin seem better than underlining, since checks do not take as much time, and, after a while, can be done rather mechanically without breaking your concentration.

When you have finished your reading, go back to the checks and reread those sections. This will reinforce your reading and help you to retain the material. You will have invoked a simple psychological principle that helps your memory.

REVIEW -- ESPECIALLY FOR SCHOOL OR BUSINESS

Your retention should be very high if, after going back to the checks immediately after reading, you go back to them again **just before** a class or meeting. You will welcome a test on the material.

IN SUMMARY (Step #5)

Improve your comprehension by:

--reading at the proper speed
--reading in the proper environment
--putting checks in the margin as you read
--reviewing before a class or meeting.

AFTERWORD

Your reading has improved and you should be proud of yourself. Keep up the words-per-minute rate you now have, or keep trying to improve. You may get rusty if you do not maintain your newly mastered reading skills. But rest assured that you will always have the skills, and whenever you choose to sharpen them, you need only review the underlinings, bold print, and summary sections of this chapter.

"Good writing is communicating. No matter how many big words or great ideas you present, if the reader does not understand what you have written, you have not communicated. Write with your audience in mind."

Dr. Edward F. Droge, Jr.

5 SIMPLE STEPS TO BETTER WRITING

by Dr. Edward F. Droge, Jr.

STEP # 1. <u>Don't Slow the Flow In The Beginning</u>.

Get the ideas down on paper or on to the computer screen. Do not worry about ANYTHING in the beginning of the writing project except to **GET THE PROJECT ITSELF UNDERWAY**. Bogging down the writing process can kill the enthusiasm and creativity necessary for writing a good piece.

One of the easiest ways to bog down the writing process is to be overly concerned with details in the beginning stages of the piece, be it a letter, a report, a composition, or any other kind of writing. For example, spelling, grammar, and punctuation are very important ingredients of good writing, but they are the kinds of ingredients that can be reviewed and changed over and over again in the middle and latter stages of the writing process; you need not become overly concerned with them in the beginning of the process. Moreover, with the technology available to us today, computers can help you to check the spelling and other details later in the revision stages.

As noted below, revision is recognized as a key to good writing, and it is during the revision stages that the writer should be concerned with spelling, grammar, punctuation, and the like. During the initial stage, however, the "first-draft" stage, the writer should be interested in getting down on paper as much of the big picture as possible, without permitting details like spelling to impede progress.

Neither should the fine-tuning of ideas be permitted to slow the flow in the initial stage of the writing. Let the thoughts flow on to the paper as quickly as they enter your mind. Fine-tuning the thoughts is important, but the revision stage is the appropriate place for that exercise.

Have you ever been writing an essay or a report of some kind, and in the middle of the process had a great thought escape you because you spent too much time worrying about details or because you attempted to refine a particular point before moving on to the next? Great thoughts are the substance of great writing and you cannot afford to let even one great thought escape.

Keep the thoughts flowing to the page as quickly as possible in the first-draft stage. Define and refine, review and revise only when the first draft is complete.

STEP # 2. <u>See The Big Picture At All Times</u>.

Many good writers use an outline to sketch the big picture before they actually engage the text of the piece. Outlines can be very helpful in seeing on paper a beginning, a middle, and an end to what the writer is about to express. Anyone who has ever written a composition knows that thoughts sometimes sound great as they reverberate in the mind, but sound odd when they actually reach the paper. Outlines can help to get the big-picture-thoughts down on paper to test their strength, and, if weak or odd, you can shift them or change them to suit.

QUESTION: What kind of outline is best to use?

ANSWER: The one that works best for the individual. You choose.

Q: How is an outline structured?

A: An outline should sketch the BIG PICTURE of what is to be said. It should, in its simplest form, sketch a beginning, a middle, and an end to the piece. If you can keep it simple, do so. For example, if the topic is "My Vacation in Rio," the outline could sketch the trip down (beginning), the stay in the city (middle), and the trip back (end).

Q: Should an outline be written in sentences or phrases or single words?

A: Whatever works best for YOU, remembering that an outline, in particular, is not a place to get bogged down with details (like: should I write this in a sentence or a phrase? Should I use numbers or letters? Capital letters?). Any form is acceptable: sentences, phrases, single words, numbers, letters -- upper case or lower case or both, or any combination of these as well. Sketch the big picture and don't permit yourself to get bogged down.

Q: Should I ignore details entirely?

A: Don't get bogged down in details like spelling, etc., but by all means flesh out the outline to be as detailed as you can make it. View it as a **blueprint**: follow it to write the piece. In the "Vacation in Rio" piece, for example, you may want to flesh out the trip down (beginning) by describing the odd driver and the hilarious taxi ride to the airport, the bumpy airplane ride through patches of clouds, the view of Rio from the air as it lay in the sun, (middle) the condition of the city and the beaches, the swimwear you noticed, the bellhop at the hotel, the night you and the other travelers got sick after a meal, (end) the interesting thing that happened on the plane ride back, the incredible coincidence of getting the same odd cab driver going home, and your thoughts in retrospect on the value of the trip.

The outline as described above could look like this:

"My Vacation in Rio"

I. The trip down (beginning)
     --the odd driver and the hilarious taxi ride to the airport
     --the bumpy airplane ride through patches of clouds
     --the view of Rio from the air as it lay in the sun

II. The stay in the city (middle)
     --the condition of the city and the beaches
     --the swimwear you noticed
     --the bellhop at the hotel
     --the night you and the other travelers got sick after a meal

III. The trip back (end)
     --the interesting thing that happened on the plane ride back
     --the incredible coincidence of getting the same odd cab driver going home.
     --your thoughts in retrospect on the value of the trip

In the end, this piece may need much work to pull it together enough to interest a reader more than, say, a home movie of your travels (and you know how boring they can get after a while), but at least the outline above has sketched the big picture in an order that makes sense. Is it the only way to outline this piece? Absolutely not. This vacation piece could be written and outlined dozens of ways. Here is another outline version, with the same essence, but using a slightly different form:

"My Vacation in Rio"

I. The trip down (beginning)
    A. to the airport
        1. the hilarious taxi ride
        2. the odd driver
    B. airplane
        1. the bumpy ride through patches of clouds
        2. the view of Rio from the air
            a. as it lay in the sun (weather)
            b. as it lay in the sun (desc. of buildings, beaches, etc.)

II. The stay in the city (middle)
    A. the condition
        1. of the city
        2. of the beaches
    B. the swimwear you noticed
    C. the bellhop at the hotel
    D. the night you and the other
travelers got sick after a meal

III. The trip back (end)
    A. the interesting thing that happened on the
plane ride back
    B. the incredible coincidence of getting the
same odd cab driver going home.
    C. your thoughts in retrospect on the value
of the trip

Perhaps you would prefer to tell the story differently. Perhaps you would construct the outline differently. Under II. B., for example, perhaps you would prefer not to talk about the swimwear. Fine. Or perhaps you would prefer to change the order of your report. Fine. It is important for **you**, the writer, to be comfortable with the outline, how it is constructed and how it will guide you to the completion of the piece.

Of course, the same story may be approached in several different ways, and, as a result, the outlines would be completely different in content, if not form. For example, you could contrast this vacation to the last vacation trip you took -- to Australia; or you could compare it to the last time you were in Rio; or you could completely ignore the rides down and back and focus exclusively on the people you met during your stay, and so on and so on and so on.

Remember, too, that outlines may change as the piece is written. If you sketch the big picture in an outline, and you are comfortable with it, but then decide as you engage in writing the piece that certain aspects should be emphasized or added, or a different approach should be taken, rest assured that it is perfectly acceptable to veer from the outline. Keep reminding yourself, however, to **keep seeing the big picture**.

Regardless of how you approach the piece, or what you feel should be emphasized, the outline should serve you as the blueprint for writing the document, establishing a beginning, a middle, and an end. Would a contractor ever attempt to build a house or a skyscraper without first carefully constructing a blueprint? Neither should a writer attempt to build a piece of writing without first carefully constructing a beginning, a middle, and an end. See the big picture and always be mindful of it as you write.

Is an outline the only way to see the big picture? No. If you have the kind of mind that is able to envision the entire piece and to retain it and to revise it without committing it to paper, then you need not use an outline. Most people, however, do not fall into this category.

Remember that the outline may be as simple or as sophisticated as you wish to make it. Writing an outline should be viewed as pleasureful and beneficial, not painful. Think of how it helps you in that it establishes the structure you will follow. Think of it as pleasureful because it makes the overall writing easier for you and gives you a much better chance of writing successfully than if you were to engage the piece without it.

REVIEW

Again, points to remember are 1. Always see the big picture -- before you engage the piece and during the writing process itself, and 2. Don't allow yourself to get bogged down in spelling, punctuation, grammar, fine-tuning ideas or the like, in the beginning, or first-draft, stage of the process. The first draft should be a smooth flow from your mind to the paper (or computer screen). Of course, if you are working from an outline, you have prepared yourself by devoting thought to the project before the first word of the piece is written.

STEP # 3. <u>State The Point Of The Piece Immediately</u>.

When I taught Writing at Harvard University, I had my students state the point of each paper in the very first sentence. By the end of the course, I would permit them the luxury of attempting to be creative enough to state it in the second or third sentence, or even in the last sentence of the first paragraph, but by no means ever were they permitted to state it later than the first paragraph. In most instances, particularly when you are attempting to improve your skills, the "point sentence" or "thesis sentence" should be the very first sentence of the piece.

Many readers -- maybe even you fall into this category -- often do not read beyond the first paragraph of a piece. Readers generally approach a piece of writing wanting to know immediately what it is about, and as much as possible about how the writer intends to treat the topic. If the reader gets to the end of the first paragraph and still does not know the specific point you are going to make in the piece, you may have missed your only opportunity to state the essence of your thoughts.

You may be thinking now that it is impossible sometimes to state the point of the piece in only one sentence. Nonsense. Simply distill what you are about to say into one clear, concise thought. Whether you are writing a 20 page report or a two page letter, your writing must have a point to make, and that point must be able to be captured in one sentence.

Let's say you are writing a report about the state of Communism in Eastern Europe today. Perhaps this is an assignment for school, or an analysis for the international trade department of your business. If you have thought out the report as you should have by the time you are ready to start writing, that is, you have established the big picture in your own mind, preferably in an outline, and the report has a beginning, a middle, and an end, then you must have a point in mind to make to your professor or to your boss and, most important, to yourself. What is it?

Is it that the fall of Communism in Eastern Europe has created an enormous, untapped market for Western businesses? Is it that the current state of affairs in Eastern Europe demonstrates conspicuously that Communism was the glue that held together the economies of the countries, and that, without it, certain countries are doomed to constant struggle? What is it exactly that you are about to describe or explain or defend in your 20 pages? Tell us, the readers, in one sentence, one clear sentence. And tell us up front, in the very first sentence of the report.

Let's say you are writing a letter to a corporation. What exactly is the point of the letter? Is it a letter to a manufacturer to complain about the defective product that you bought? Do you want your money back? Do you want to exchange the product for a new one? Do you want neither of those, but only the satisfaction of knowing that you have brought this matter to the attention of the company? Does the defect cause a safety problem that may jeopardize others? How seriously? What is it exactly that you want to say?

Whatever it is, distill the message into one clear sentence and state it in the beginning of the letter. You will know then for certain that the reader has been exposed to the essence of your thoughts, whether he or she reads the entire letter or not. Go on, of course, to explain or describe or argue your point further in the letter, but do not fail to state it in the first sentence.

The "point sentence" or "thesis sentence" serves two important functions: first, it forces **you** to think carefully about exactly what you want to say, and, second, it presents that thought to the reader immediately to help him or her understand better what is about to be read. Your thesis, your

opinion, your argument, your description --
whatever it is that you want to say -- can and should
be distilled into one sentence and placed in the
beginning of the piece. If you cannot put the
essence of your thoughts into one sentence, then you
may not have a point to make, and if that is so, then
you may not have a reader interested enough to
engage the piece, at least beyond the first paragraph.

STEP # 4. <u>Tell Them What You Are Going To Say.</u>

<u>Say It.</u>

<u>Tell Them What You Said.</u>

This is a tried and true method of writing, a method that is certain to give you ample opportunity to be understood. Think about writing for a moment: what is it? Why do we write? Yes, to **communicate** our thoughts to others. Though a writer also may derive therapeutic or cathartic benefits from the process, if no one reads the writing, or, if the reader does not understand what is written, then the writer has not communicated.

Tell Them What You Are Going To Say.

All good writing needs a beginning, a middle, and an end. With the point of the piece stated in the first paragraph, the beginning is established. In essence, what you accomplish in the first paragraph is to tell the reader what you are going to be expounding on in the middle of the piece.

Say It.

In the middle of the piece, the good writer provides significant support or description or explanation of the point that was stated in the opening paragraph. For example, if the point of your piece is that the decline of Communism in Europe has devastated the economy of countries x, y, and z, then that is a contention that needs support. Just because you say something is so does not mean that it is true or that the reader will believe it; you need to support what you say.

If, in the Communism piece, you were to provide indisputable statistics that clearly demonstrate that the economy slipped in countries x, y, and z after the decline of Communism, it would be difficult for the reader not to understand your point and to give it due credibility.

If the topic of a different piece is the environment, and, let's say, your point concerns the harmful effects that the average person can have on the environment, you must provide ample evidence in the middle of the piece to support your point. It would be difficult, for example, for the reader to dispute hard evidence from scientific studies that show the effect of aerosol sprays on the ozone layer.

If your piece is descriptive, the middle, understandably, is the appropriate place for the description. Let's say the point of your piece concerns the architectural beauty that generally goes unnoticed in a certain city. In the middle of the piece you would need to provide ample examples of architectural highlights in that city -- perhaps you would describe the flying buttresses of a particular church, or the intricate cornice work on particular office buildings, or the bas relief on certain other buildings.

If you are writing an explanative essay -- let's say you are explaining how a battery works -- it would be necessary for you to provide ample, understandable details in the middle of the piece. Perhaps you would want to create an image that non-scientific minds could easily understand: picture, for example, that there is a pipe that runs through the middle of the battery from end to end. The pipe is just wide enough to accept golf balls. Now picture yourself loading golf balls into the pipe, one after the other, and, as you load one in, it pushes the other balls before it deeper and deeper into the battery, until, eventually, the first golf ball loaded exits the other end of the pipe. This, you could point out, represents the flow of electricity through a battery, with the golf balls representing electrons.

The more attention you pay to explaining the process in the middle of the piece, the more appreciative the reader will be, and the more likely that the reader will understand your explanation, which is, of course, the goal of your writing.

Tell Them What You Said

What about the end? Good writers know that readers generally remember the end of a piece more readily than any other part. To leave a piece without proper closure is to leave the reader unsatisfied, perhaps with a sense that your writing is incomplete, which, in effect, clouds your credibility and jeopardizes your success.

The end must relate to the middle and to the beginning, and the simplest, most effective method of ending a piece successfully is to present a brief summary of what you said and to draw a conclusion that repeats the point stated in the opening sentence.

Remember that summarizing is not the same as simply repeating. An effective summary is brief, containing only key words and phrases from the body of the piece. A summary should be complete, that is, covering all points made in the body, but it should not be a lengthy repetition. A good summary **distills** the information presented above into prominent pieces that fit together into a one- or two-

or three-sentence foundation that supports the point that was stated in the beginning.

For example, in your Communism piece, you may wish to close by summarizing the facts demonstrated by the statistics you provided: "As the statistics clearly demonstrate in countries x, y, and z, after the demise of Communism, unemployment rose, the gross national product declined, and inflation more than quadrupled." This easily flows into the final sentence, which reaffirms the point stated in the opening paragraph: "There can be no doubt that the fall of Communism in these countries contributed significantly to the devastation of their economies."

By sandwiching your argument or explanation or description between a "point/thesis" sentence and a summary, you offer yourself three opportunities to communicate with the reader.

STEP # 5. <u>Revise, Revise, Revise</u>.

There are two kinds of writers in the world: "Mozartians" and "Beethovenites." Mozartians, like Mozart, can write the first draft of a piece from beginning to end, with minimal revision required in the process. The Beethovenites, like Beethoven, need to revise the first draft of a piece over and over before it could be considered a respectable first draft. Please note I am talking about first drafts; both composers, though brilliant, knew that their writing would require revision stages after the first draft was completed.

Whether you classify yourself as a Mozartian or Beethovenite, when you write your first draft, do so knowing full well that you will need to review it and revise it several times before it can be appreciated by others. The revision stages should be viewed as **opportunities** to fine tune a piece and to make any corrections and improvements required.

Whether or not you revise in your mind as you write, you will be well served to write a first draft and then revise it and then revise that draft and then revise that draft and then keep revising until you are comfortable that you no longer can improve the piece significantly. If you have been accustomed to writing a piece from beginning to end in a first draft, feeling that revising was not necessary, feeling

comfortable that the first draft is the best writing
you can offer, I suggest that you change your way of
thinking immediately if you sincerely wish to write
well.

Every English teacher to have stepped into a
classroom has had a fair share of students who hand
in compositions without even bothering to revise.
You can be sure that those are not the "A" students.

Some writers may need to revise less than
others, but every piece requires a review and
revision. Even if the thoughts are well articulated,
there may very well be a misspelling or
typographical error. Humans make mistakes.

The Secret To Successful Revision

Virtually every product we buy has been
tested extensively before it reaches the store. From
food products to sunglasses to automobiles,
manufacturers test the quality and form of the
product and marketing analysts test the expected
public response to the product. After all,
manufacturers are in business to make money, and if
the product does not sell, it becomes a financial loss
for the manufacturer and it will no longer be
produced, thus failing to achieve the goal the
manufacturer had in mind when the product was
launched.

The inherent goal that the writer has in mind when he or she launches a piece is, simply put, to communicate thoughts successfully to the reader. If the reader cannot understand the piece, it cannot be considered successful.

What, then, is the best method of testing for success before the writing product is ultimately launched? **Let readers read it, and pay attention carefully to what they say about it.**

When I taught Writing at Harvard, I used peer review in the writing instruction process. Students were divided into groups of three and shared their assigned essays in draft stages. Each student reviewed the papers of the two other members of the group and also received feedback on his or her own writing from those same two group members. This exercise was well received by the students and proved an invaluable tool for them in successfully revising their papers.

One concern that usually arose in the beginning of the course was voiced by students who felt that their ability to write was superior to the others in their group: therefore, what could be gained by getting feedback from inferior writers. And, in general, how could any student be expected to have enough expertise in writing to offer feedback that had a significant level of credibility for the writer?

The concern was quickly dispelled when I clarified the concept: no student was expected to have significant expertise as a writer. How well or how poorly a student wrote did not weigh on the task assigned, which was to read the paper and offer comments on how successful the paper communicated. The expertise expected of the peer reviewers was simply as a **reader**, and, if the peer reviewer discovered parts of the paper that were difficult to read or understand -- for whatever reason -- they were to point out those parts. Since the purpose of writing is to communicate to the reader, the writer had to respect the comments of the peer reviewer, though they were not forced to accept them.

The peer reviewers were not to make judgments. They were only to offer their **reactions as readers**. In other words, the peer reviewers were not to judge whether any particular part of the paper was good or bad writing, but, rather, only to make comments that reflected whether or not the reader understood a particular point or if the reader stumbled over a particular section.

If a reader says to you: "this is bad writing," then the reader is making a judgment and is setting himself or herself up as an expert in writing. If, on the other hand, a reader says to you: "I don't understand this point," or "I am confused here about what you are trying to say," then the reader is merely giving you feedback as a reader. The successful writer will pay attention to feedback from readers.

To be successful in everything you write, you should revise, revise, revise. Most important, however, you should build into your writing process a revision stage that includes getting feedback from readers.

Give your piece to family or friends or co-workers. Ask them to let you know if they notice any parts that are not clear or that seem tangled, or confusing, or incomplete. While they are at it, they may also notice spelling errors or typos. Be clear, however, that you would appreciate it if they did not necessarily make judgments about the writing: you are interested in their opinions as readers more than their opinions as writers. Be candid with them and ask them to avoid using any terms that indicate bad writing -- to say something is bad writing is to make a judgment. Ask them to confine their comments to how they were able to read the piece from beginning to end. Were there any parts where they stumbled? Were there any parts that were confusing?

You should be patient with those who agree to help you by reading your writing and offering feedback. It may take a while for them to give you what you seek. But once you are able to share your writing regularly with a group of readers, you will increase your chances of writing successfully if you pay attention carefully to what they say, and revise accordingly.

Writing well is within your grasp. You can do it. Get excited about your writing.

Why not write something now.

5 SIMPLE STEPS TO QUICK AND POWERFUL MATH

by Dr. Edward F. Droge, Jr.

STEP # 1. Simplify Numbers

The easier the numbers are to work with, the more quickly and more easily you will be able to arrive at the solutions to math problems. If, for example, you were adding 36 and 100, it should present little difficulty to arrive at the sum of 136. But if you were adding 38 to 98, you may encounter a bit more difficulty and you probably would take a longer time to arrive at the solution, which is, of course, also 136.

The goal you must set for yourself is to simplify numbers, that is, to see them in relation to numbers that are easy to work with. Numbers that are easy to work with in math are numbers ending in 0, 00, 000, and so on. The number 20, for example, is easier to work with than the number 19 or the number 21. Adding the numbers 20 and 17 to arrive at the sum of 37 is easier than adding the numbers 19 and 18, which also equal 37.

Using the numbers in the addition problems above, most people would acknowledge that working with 100 and 36 is easier than working with 98 and 38, and working with 20 and 17 is easier than working with 19 and 18, but those same people would think they have little control over solving a problem if the numbers given to them were 98 and 38 or 19 and 18. *But that's where you will set yourself apart: by recognizing that you do have control to make the problem easier by simplifying the numbers.*

If you were to train yourself to see that 19 plus 18 is the same as 20 plus 17, you would be able to solve the problem faster and easier because you would be working with easier numbers. Obviously, then, you need to train yourself to simplify.

Follow a simple rule: **when possible, change one of the numbers in the problem to a number that ends with 0 or 00 or 000**. For example, in the addition of 19 and 18, change the 19 to 20. By doing so, however, you must change the other number to compensate for the simplification, in this case, by changing the 18 to 17.

Here's the rule for **addition** (the rule for subtraction is described later):

IN AN **ADDITION** PROBLEM, IF YOU SIMPLIFY ONE NUMBER BY **INCREASING** IT, YOU MUST **DECREASE ANOTHER NUMBER** BY THE SAME AMOUNT; **IF YOU DECREASE TO SIMPLIFY**, YOU MUST **INCREASE ANOTHER NUMBER** IN THE SAME AMOUNT. In other words, if you change 19 to 20, you have INCREASED it by 1; you must then DECREASE the other number by 1: thus the 18 becomes 17.

If the numbers you were to add were 21 and 16, you would want to change the 21 to 20 by subtracting 1. Following the rule, you would then add 1 to the other number; thus, the 16 then becomes 17. In other words, adding 21 and 16 is the same as adding 20 and 17.

Let's look at the other sample problem above. If you wanted to add 98 to 38, you would see that 98 is close enough to 100 to convert it without much effort, since you would want to work with 100 rather than 98. If you convert it, however, you must also convert the other number in the problem: if you add 2 to 98, you must then subtract 2 from the other number, that is, the 38 becomes 36.

When you work with this simplifying principle long enough to master it, you will look at a problem such as adding 98 and 38, and you will see it immediately as the same as adding 100 and 36, and you will know instantly that 98 and 38 are 136. Those around you will still be working it out and will be astonished at how quickly you arrived at the answer.

Again, the rule for simplification is:

IN AN **ADDITION** PROBLEM, IF YOU SIMPLIFY ONE NUMBER BY **INCREASING** IT, YOU MUST **DECREASE ANOTHER NUMBER** BY THE SAME AMOUNT; **IF YOU DECREASE TO SIMPLIFY**, YOU MUST **INCREASE ANOTHER NUMBER** IN THE SAME AMOUNT.

Here are more examples:

NUMBERS TO BE ADDED = SIMPLIFIED

12+37 = 10+39 (SUBTRACT 2 from 12 to get 10; ADD 2 to 37)

33+154 = 30+157 (SUBTRACT 3; ADD 3)

203+154 = 200+157 (SUBTRACT 3; ADD 3)

97+67 = 100+64 (ADD 3 to 97 to get 100; SUBTRACT 3 from 67)

48+63 = 50+61 (ADD 2; SUBTRACT 2)

SUBTRACTION

The rule for simplification in **subtraction** is similar but not the same. Just remember to change two numbers equally:

IN A **SUBTRACTION** PROBLEM, IF YOU SIMPLIFY ONE NUMBER BY **INCREASING** IT, YOU MUST **ALSO INCREASE ANOTHER NUMBER** BY THE SAME AMOUNT; **IF YOU DECREASE TO SIMPLIFY**, YOU MUST **ALSO DECREASE ANOTHER NUMBER** IN THE SAME AMOUNT.

Examples:

103 - 28 = 100 - 25 (SUBTRACT 3; SUBTRACT 3) to get 75

343 - 98 = 345 - 100 (ADD 2; ADD 2) to get 245

196 - 71 = 200 - 75 (ADD 4; ADD 4) to get 125

STEP # 2. <u>Think Money ($$$)</u>

Since we use money virtually every day of
our lives, we become accustomed to adding and
subtracting in terms of dollars and cents. We can
use that familiarity with money to our advantage
when we add and subtract at any time if we simply
think of the numbers in terms of dollars and cents.

Let's take an example: if you were asked to
add 932 and 843, it would probably take longer than
if you were asked to add $9.32 to $8.43. Right?
(The answer, of course, is $17.75 or 1775.)

If, in a problem like this, you need only
estimate the sum, that is, get only a "ballpark"
figure, it immediately helps to know that nine dollars
and change added to eight dollars and change will
give you seventeen dollars and change. No?

In our daily lives, we also are likely to be
much more careful with our addition or subtraction
when it involves money, and, so, why not convert all
(or as many as possible) of our addition and
subtraction problems into money terms in our minds.

It follows, then, that not only will we find the
problems simpler, but also we will be more careful
with them.

Here are more examples:

THINK DOLLARS AND CENTS

327 + 523   OR $3.27 + $5.23 = $8.50 (or 850)

If you think vertically:

	327		$3.27
	523	OR	$5.23
	850		$8.50

Again, if an estimate is all you need: three dollars and change plus five dollars and change will give you eight dollars and change.

The simplicity benefits should be even more apparent with larger numbers:

2345 + 2213   OR $23.45 + $22.13 = $45.58 (or 4558)

14766 + 2020   OR $147.66 + $20.20 = $167.86 (or 16786)

Try subtraction:

14766 - 2020   OR $147.66 - $20.20 = $127.46 (or 12746)

If only an estimate is needed, think of having $147 and giving away $20. How much would you have left? (But remember that there is change involved.)

<u>AMAZE</u> <u>YOUR</u> <u>FRIENDS</u>

Our brains are such powerful tools, and far too often we do not use the power. With this approach to math problems, that is, thinking in terms of dollars and cents, we can tap the power of our brains and do much, or all, of the math in our head.

Ask a friend to give you a 5-digit number and a 4-digit number to add or subtract (as in the example above: 14766 + or - 2020). Let your friend use a pencil and paper, while you do the math in your head. If you have mastered this approach, you will have the answer before your friend does.

If you get really good at this, you can let your friend use a calculator and you will still have the answer first, especially if you only need to estimate or arrive at a "ballpark" figure.

STEP # 3. <u>A QUICK TRICK ("Q-T")</u>

Multiplying by 11

I gave a speech to several hundred students and their teachers at a school once and amazed the entire audience with a demonstration of a simple time-saver in multiplication.

I asked six students to join me at the microphone, and I gave a different student in the audience a calculator to use in the demonstration. I separated the six students into two groups of three.

In Group 1 I asked the first student to say aloud a number from one to fifty. He said thirty-six. Immediately I turned to the first student in Group 2 and asked him to remember the following number: three hundred ninety six.

I asked the second student in Group 1 for a number from fifty-one to one hundred. She said ninety-three. Immediately I turned to the second student in Group 2 and asked her to remember the following number: one thousand twenty three.

I asked the third student in Group 1 for any number between one hundred and one thousand. She said three hundred forty five. Immediately I turned to the third student in Group 2 and asked him to remember the following number: three thousand seven hundred ninety five.

I then asked the student in the audience with the calculator to multiply each number offered by a student in Group 1 by 11. I asked the first student in Group 1 to repeat the number loud enough for all to hear. The number was thirty six.

While the student with the calculator punched in 36 x 11, I turned to the first student in Group 2 and asked him to repeat the number I had asked him to remember -- loud, really loud, so that everyone could hear it. He said three hundred ninety six.

I asked the student with the calculator what he had come up with as the product of 36 x 11. Shout it out, I said. Three hundred ninety six, he shouted.

The audience was a mixture of "ooh" and "wow" and the like, and then they broke into applause, appreciating the speed at which I had been able to multiply two numbers in my head.

I asked the second student in Group 1 to repeat her number: ninety-three, she said. I pointed to the student with the calculator, signaling him to multiply it by eleven, then before he could come up with the answer, I turned to the second student in Group 2 and asked for the number I had given her: one thousand twenty three, she shouted. I pointed to the student with the calculator: one thousand twenty three, he shouted.

More "oohs" and "wows" came from the audience, louder this time, and then more applause.

I asked the third student in Group 1 for her number: three hundred forty five, she shouted. I pointed to the student with the calculator and he punched away. I turned to the third student in Group 2 and he shouted "three thousand seven hundred ninety five." Without much of a cue needed, the student with the calculator rang out his answer: "three thousand seven hundred ninety five."

The audience cheered and clapped. They stood. They hooted and yelled in appreciation. For one brief moment, I was a hero.

It was so simple.

YOU CAN MULTIPLY BY ELEVEN SO QUICKLY YOU WILL AMAZE PEOPLE

It may seem difficult to multiply two numbers in your head, but it is really very simple.

Here is the secret:

When you multiply by 11, you simply add the digits of the number and insert the sum in the middle.

For example: 11 x 36

add the 3 and the 6 to get 9

insert the 9 between the 3 and the 6 to get 396

11 x 36 = 396

It's that simple.

Here's another example: 11 x 44

add the 4 and the 4 to get 8

insert the 8 between the 4 and the 4 to get 484

11 x 44 = 484

Here are more for you to try:

a. 11 x 27
b. 11 x 51
c. 11 x 80
d. 11 x 16

(answers: a. 297; b. 561; c. 880; d. 176)

Practice this for a while and you will be able to multiply in your head with amazing speed.

What if the numbers added together equal 10 or more?

Let's use my second example in the school demonstration above: 11 x 93

add the 9 and the 3 to get 12

insert the 2, carry the 1

add the 1 to the 9 to get 10

11 x 93 = 1023 (i.e. 10-2-3)

Try another: 11 x 78

  add the 7 and 8 to get 15

  insert the 5, carry the 1

  add the 1 to the 7 to get 8

11 x 78 = 858 (i.e. 8-5-8)

Here are more:

a. 11 x 68
b. 11 x 39
c. 11 x 99
d. 11 x 74

(answers: a. 748; b 429; c. 1089; d. 814)

Now let's try three-digit numbers.

Using my third example from the school
demonstration above: 11 x 345

> The rule for three or more digits is to
add and insert from the right, thus

> starting from the right, add 5 to the 4
to get 9

> insert the 9

> add the 4 to the 3 to get 7

> insert the 7

11 x 345 = 3795

Note that the numbers on each end of 345 have
remained (that is, the 3 and the 5), but the middle
digit (that is, the 4) has been replaced by the
insertions.

Let's try another: 11 x 421

> starting from the right, add the 1 to
the 2 to get 3

> insert the 3

> add the 2 to the 4 to get 6

insert the 6

11 x 421 = 4631

Again, note that the numbers on each end of 421 have remained (that is, the 4 and the 1), but the middle digit (that is, the 2) has been replaced by the insertions.

The larger the numbers, the more practice you will need to master this approach, but, remember, **once mastered, you will be able to save time and amaze everyone.**

Here are more samples for practice (remember to insert and carry if the addition ever comes to ten or more):

a. 11 x 816
b. 11 x 542
c. 11 x 173
d. 11 x 985

(answers: a. 8976; b. 5962; c. 1903; d. 10835)

STEP # 4. <u>ANOTHER "Q-T" (QUICK TRICK)</u>

Multiplying by 5

I wish I had a dollar for the number of times I have had to multiply by 5 in my life. I think, for example, of all the times I have bought 5 units of the same item at the supermarket or at a department store. (Dog or cat owners who buy food for the week can probably identify with me here.)

Before I buy anything, especially when paying in cash, I prefer to know before I get to the register how much I am going to need when I check out. If I am buying 5 units of the same item, therefore, I need to multiply the unit price by 5 to arrive at the total cost. Before employing the easy way to multiply by 5, it normally took me a while to arrive at the answer. Now, however, it's a snap.

Here's the secret:

First, let me offer a brief explanation of why the method works. The explanation also will help you to remember the method.

Multiplying a number by 1 is the same as taking the WHOLE number. Multiplying a number by .5, therefore, is the same as taking HALF of the number, right?

Thus, to multiply a number by .5 is the same as to divide the number in half, that is, to divide it by 2.

Let's try it:
$$26$$
$$\underline{\text{x .5}}$$
$$13.0$$

Half of 26, or 26 divided by 2, equals 13

Another example:

$$1246$$
$$\underline{\text{x .5}}$$
$$623.0$$

Half of 1246, or 1246 divided by 2, equals 623

Taking half of a number is easy, isn't it? (Here is how your mind may have approached it: half of 12 is **6**; half of 4 is **2**; half of 6 is **3**)

It is easier simply to take half of 26 (13) or half of 1246 (623) to arrive at the answers, than it is to multiply by .5. Dividing by 2 is not all that difficult or complicated, and, certainly, if calculating in our heads, dividing by 2 is much simpler than multiplying by .5.

If the number to be multiplied by .5 is an odd number, the principle is the same.

For example:

$$\begin{array}{r} 27 \\ \times\,.5 \\ \hline 13.5 \end{array}$$

Half of 27, or 27 divided by 2, equals 13.5

Another example:

$$\begin{array}{r} 445 \\ \times\,.5 \\ \hline 222.5 \end{array}$$

Half of 445, or 445 divided by 2, equals 222.5

So here is the first fundamental principle:

MULTIPLYING BY .5 IS THE SAME AS DIVIDING BY 2.

Since the number 5 is actually ten times greater than .5 (10 x .5 = 5), the principle for multiplying by 5 is the same as the principle for multiplying by .5 except that you simply must add a zero to the number (which is the same as having multiplied it by 10).

In other words, **when you want to multiply a number by 5, simply add a zero to the number and then divide by 2.**

For example: How much is 2486 times 5?

Conventional method:

$$\begin{array}{r} 2486 \\ \times\ \ \ 5 \\ \hline 12430 \end{array}$$

Easier method -- You can do this in your head:

Add a zero to 2486, making it 24860. Half of 24860, or 24860 divided by 2, equals 12430.

(Here is how your mind may approach it: half of 24 is **12**; half of 8 is **4**; half of 60 is **30**.)

It makes no difference if the number to be multiplied is odd or even.

For example: How much is 243 times 5?

Conventional method:

$$243$$
$$\underline{\times \ 5}$$
$$1215$$

Easier method -- do it in your head:

Add a zero to 243, making it 2430. Half of 2430, or 2430 divided by 2, equals 1215

(Here is how you may approach it: Half of 24 is **12**; half of 30 is **15**. This is the kind of calculation you can do in your head, no?)

So, here is the principle to follow:

WHEN YOU WANT TO MULTIPLY A NUMBER BY 5, SIMPLY ADD A ZERO TO THE NUMBER AND THEN DIVIDE BY 2.

Perhaps you want to multiply a number by 50 or 500. No problem. Same fundamental principle with slight, logical variations.

WHEN YOU WANT TO MULTIPLY A NUMBER BY 50, SIMPLY ADD TWO ZEROES TO THE NUMBER AND THEN DIVIDE BY 2.

WHEN YOU WANT TO MULTIPLY A NUMBER BY 500, SIMPLY ADD THREE ZEROES TO THE NUMBER AND THEN DIVIDE BY 2.

For example:

$$\begin{array}{r} 648 \\ \underline{\times 50} \\ 32400 \end{array}$$

OR

Add two zeroes to 648, making it 64800, and then divide by 2. Half of 64800, or 64800 divided by 2, equals 32400.

Let's try 500:

$$\begin{array}{r} 865 \\ \underline{\times 500} \\ 432500 \end{array}$$

OR

Add three zeroes to 865, making it 865000, and then divide by 2. Half of 865000, or 865000 divided by 2, equals 432500.

Just a little practice with this method should permit you to master it entirely. You may never use the conventional method when you need to multiply by .5 or 5 or 50 or 500 again. Why do so, when it is so much easier to add some zeroes, if necessary, and then divide by 2?

Do you think your friends and relatives would be impressed if you asked them to give you a number, and then you were able to multiply that number by 50 or 500 in your head more quickly than they could by using paper and pencil, or, perhaps, even a calculator?

STEP # 5. <u>YET ANOTHER "Q-T"</u>

PERCENTAGES

Quick, what is 20% of 45? What is 25% of 44? What is 33 1/3% of 96? What is 50% of 28?

You can save time if you know that **taking 20% of a number is the same as dividing the number by 5.**

Taking 25% of a number is the same as dividing the number by 4.

Taking 33 1/3% of a number is the same as dividing the number by 3.

Taking 50% of a number is the same as dividing the number by 2.

Thus, in the examples given above, 20% of 45 (think 45 divided by 5). Answer: 9.

25% of 44 (think 44 divided by 4). Answer: 11.

33 1/3% of 96 (think 96 divided by 3). Answer: 32.

50% of 28 (think 28 divided by 2). Answer: 14.

The advantage of thinking like this becomes conspicuous when the numbers are larger. For example:

20% of 1585   (think 1585 divided by 5). Answer: 317.

(You may approach it by thinking: 15 divided by 5 is **3**; 8 divided by 5 is **1**, with 3 remaining; 35 divided by 5 is **7**.)

Obviously, these alternative methods for finding percentages operate more easily when the numbers are evenly divisible by 2, 3, 4, or 5, depending on the percentage you are looking for. Certainly, however, even if the numbers being used are not evenly divisible, these methods will give you **estimates** very quickly.

Again:

Percentage Sought	Divide By
20%	**5**
25%	**4**
33 1/3%	**3**
50%	**2**

"We use merely a fraction of the brain power available to us. With just a little effort and a good technique, we can amaze ourselves and others. Our brain will permit us to do wondrous things, wondrous things."

Dr. Edward F. Droge, Jr.

5 SIMPLE STEPS TO AMAZING POWERS OF MEMORY

by Dr. Edward F. Droge, Jr.

Did you ever get home from grocery shopping and realize that you forgot to buy something you had intended to buy? Did you ever meet someone and then forget his or her name? Did you ever have to speak before a group and then leave out an important point you had wanted to make? Did you ever forget a telephone number?

Chances are good that you answered "yes" to more than one of the above questions. We all forget from time to time. Right?

Well, maybe not. How would you like to increase your memory power enough to be able to answer "no" from now on to all of the above questions? How would you like to be able to amaze your friends and relatives and others with your extraordinary memory power? How would you like to remember a telephone number virtually forever after hearing it only once? How would you like to be introduced to a dozen people at a meeting or at a party and to be able to use their names when you say goodbye to them?

WHAT THIS CAN DO FOR YOU

What do you suppose people will think of you if they know you possess amazing powers of memory? These amazing powers of memory are within your grasp. And they are not complex or difficult.

When you master the simple techniques below, you will have taken on an ability that will permit you to remember as you have never remembered before, and no one will look at you the same way again. More important, you will not look at yourself in the same way. If you know your memory power is great, what do you suppose will happen to your confidence and self esteem?

STEP # 1. <u>MEMORY CHALLENGE?</u> <u>CURE IT.</u>

CURE (**C**onnections: **U**nlikely, **R**idiculous, **E**xtraordinary)

Connections, connections, connections.

Make connections between the items to be remembered.

But not just any connections: **<u>unlikely</u>**, **<u>ridiculous</u>**, **<u>extraordinary</u>** connections.

This is the key to great memory.

We forget most often because we have not actively and aggressively made the things to be remembered stand out in our minds. It is only natural. After all, how excited do we normally get over the grocery list?

But the brain is capable of so much more than we ask of it. The brain stores virtually everything we see and hear and think. The information does not disappear from the brain; it is not erased. It is stored, waiting to be retrieved.

Unfortunately, however, the data sits in storage, like information stored on the hard disk of a computer, unable to be retrieved unless the user knows how to do it.

As we all know, it can be quite frustrating at times, trying to retrieve a piece of information, like a name or a fact or an item on a grocery list. Ever watch a quiz show on television, and get frustrated when you know the answer to a question -- you know you know it -- but it just will not come to the surface of your mind? It is buried in your memory bank.

We all have experienced that kind of frustration at one time or another. We know we know it, but we simply cannot bring it to the surface. Sometimes it is on "the tip of the tongue." Right? All it needs is a trigger, some device that will bring the information to the surface. **An unlikely, ridiculous, or extraordinary connection is exactly the device that will trigger the information virtually every time.**

If you have a memory problem: CURE it.

Here is what to do:

Connect each item to be remembered to the next item in the sequence, but connect them in an unlikely, ridiculous, or extraordinary manner. For example, let us say that you want to remember the following five items: **mouse, baseball, false eyelashes, beer, skirt**. CURE each item with the next.

It is important to connect in pairs. It reduces any number of items to be remembered into having to remember only one item, which will trigger the one with which it is paired, which will trigger the one with which it is paired, and so on and so on and so on.

Most important is that YOU make the connections that work for YOU, since the connections need to be retrieved by you, and need to stand out in your mind, not mine or anyone else's. I will offer my connections as examples, but YOUR connections will work best for YOU.

Okay, you have to remember the five items above. CURE in pairs. One way to connect mouse to baseball would be to make a mental picture of a mouse with a baseball on its head. Or a mouse with a baseball in its mouth. The idea is to make the connection as unlikely or ridiculous or extraordinary as you can -- a connection that will stand out in your mind. You are not likely to forget an image of a mouse with a baseball on its head, are you?

Now that you have mouse CURED with baseball, now you must CURE baseball with false eyelashes. Imagine, for example, a baseball with a face that has a prominent feature -- false eyelashes. Or picture in your mind a woman's face with false eyelashes and balanced on each eyelash is a baseball. Ridiculous? Right. And that is exactly what we want.

Now CURE false eyelashes to beer. Let's conjure up the mental picture of false eyelashes floating in a mug of beer. Or a bottle of beer wearing false eyelashes.

Now CURE beer to skirt. Let's picture a skirt with a pattern of little cans of beer on it. Or, perhaps, a bartender pulling the spigot to draw a frothy beer, but instead out come a steady stream of skirts.

Get the idea? Unlikely, ridiculous, extraordinary connections. In pairs. It does not matter how many items you need to remember, since you will remember them only two at a time, and you will always be able to remember all the items by simply recalling each pair at a time.

Take just a minute to review the CURES above. You will amaze yourself at how well you will remember the items.

Try it. If I say mouse, what do you think of? Baseball, right? And did that baseball have a face with something prominent? Right: false eyelashes.

This method also permits you to remember items in reverse order as well. For example, if I say skirt, what do you think of? Beer, right?

ANOTHER OPTION

If you have the kind of a mind that likes to create stories, then you can take this CURE method a step further. Connect in pairs, and weave the pairs into a story.

For example, another way to make the connections of the five items to be remembered may be:

A **mouse** is up at bat in a baseball game. He hits the **baseball**.

This is ridiculous, I know. But that is the point. My mind -- and I suspect that your mind is capable of the same -- can picture a mouse in a baseball uniform. In fact, this is a baseball game being played by two teams of mice. The pitcher mouse throws the baseball and the hitter mouse hits

it. I have connected **mouse** and **baseball** in a way
that I am unlikely to forget BECAUSE IT IS SO
RIDICULOUS.

Now to connect baseball and false eyelashes.
Easy enough. My mind ZOOMS IN (zooming in is
a useful and important technique) on the **baseball** as
it is flying through the air, and, as in a TV cartoon,
the baseball has a face on it, and the most prominent
feature: **false eyelashes**. Come on, let yourself go.
You can picture it, can't you? Believe me, the more
ridiculous the better in trying to make connections
that you will remember.

Okay, now to connect false eyelashes with
beer. Simple enough: the false **eyelashes** are
floating in **beer**, since the ball went flying into the
stands and landed in some guy's cup of beer. Can
you picture a baseball with a face on it with false
eyelashes and the false eyelashes are floating in the
beer? Are you likely to forget something as weird as
that? I doubt it, and, if not, then you are not likely
to forget the two items either: false eyelashes and
beer.

Now for the last two items. The spectator
with the beer is a burly man, but he is wearing a
skirt. The impact of the ball into his beer has spilled
some **beer** on the **skirt**. Spilling beer on a skirt is

not so extraordinary, but it is if the skirt is on a burly man, no?

In seconds, in my mind I have made a series of unlikely, ridiculous, extraordinary connections, two at a time, and I have connected the five items together.

A **mouse** is up at bat in a baseball game. He hits the **baseball**.

The **baseball** has a face on it, and the face has **false eyelashes**.

The **baseball with false eyelashes** flies into the stands and lands in the **beer** of a burly male spectator, and the **false eyelashes** are now floating in the **beer**.

The **beer** spills all over the **skirt** the man is wearing.

I have made the ridiculous connections necessary to trigger those five items for me at any time I need them. Moreover, I now can remember them in reverse order, also, if I wish, since I have connected them two at a time.

For example, as soon as I think of the **skirt**, I think of the **beer** spilled on it. As soon as I think of the **beer**, I think of the **false eyelashes** floating in it.

As soon as I think of the **false eyelashes**, I think of the face on the **baseball**.

As soon as I think of the **baseball**, I think of the **mouse** who hit it.

Even if I remembered only one of the five items, and if it were somewhere in the middle of the sequence, I would still be able to remember all five items by remembering the connections on each side. See for yourself: Think of the **false eyelashes**. What are the items on each side? Right. **Baseball** and **beer**.

Close your eyes and try to remember all five items again.

Congratulations.

It's simple, isn't it? And oh so powerful.

You do not need to make a story out of the items. In fact, for some people this would be too difficult. I offer the method only as one more option. To CURE in pairs is most important; you need no story

Now that you have the idea of how to CURE, let's try a list of 10!!!!

STEP # 2. <u>REMEMBERING LISTS</u>

Never forget another item at the grocery store. CURE the list. You have already CURED a list of five items; a grocery list of 10 items can be CURED in the same way.

Okay, here are the 10 items you want to buy: **bread, shampoo, cereal, diapers, lettuce, bacon, milk, batteries, cookies, magazine**.

Remember, YOUR CURES are what will make YOU remember this grocery list, but for the purposes of demonstration, I will offer mine. Please try to make your own CURES as we move along. Use mine at any time if it works for you, but also try to create your own, just to engage the process more intimately.

Bread and shampoo. Imagine a loaf of bread with one end of it frothy and bubbly, as if it were in the shower.

Shampoo and cereal. A bowl of shampoo bottles. I have opened the box of cereal and poured out little bottles of shampoo into the bowl.

Cereal and diapers. The box of cereal is standing straight up. Your baby, in her diapers, is balancing herself upside down on top of the box of cereal.

Diapers and lettuce. There is lettuce sprouting from your baby's diaper.

Lettuce and bacon. Picture a pig -- its head is not that of an ordinary pig, however, but instead it has a head of lettuce.

Bacon and milk. You are frying bacon and into the frying pan you pour milk. (Yuk.) The milk bubbles and the bacon floats.

Milk and batteries. You are milking a cow and out of the udders come batteries.

Batteries and cookies. Chocolate chip batteries. You take the box of cookies from the shelf and see that in the box are not cookies, but batteries instead -- chocolate chip batteries.

Cookies and magazine. You know how annoying it is when you leaf through a magazine and those subscription cards fall out on to your lap. Imagine that you are leafing through a magazine and cookies keep falling out of it on to your lap.

There you have it, a list of 10 grocery items. Do you know it? Let's see.

Think of one item that you know you would need. Let's say milk. Okay, what else do you think of?

Immediately I think of milking a cow and batteries coming out of the udders. Aha! Batteries.

But I know that milk is somewhere in the middle of the list, which means that there is another CURE. Yes. Bubbling milk in a frying pan, with bacon floating in it. Aha! Bacon.

From there I can proceed in both directions to remember my CURES and cover the entire 10 items. Of course, if I simply remember the first item -- in this case, bread -- I can proceed in the order I CURED. **Bread** with bubbling **shampoo** on one end; a bowl of shampoo bottles that came from a box of **cereal**; a box of cereal with a baby in **diapers** balanced on top; **lettuce** is sprouting from the diapers; a head of lettuce sits on a pig's body (**bacon**); bacon floating in a frying pan of **milk**; milking a cow and **batteries** coming from the udders; chocolate chip batteries -- aha! **cookies**; cookies keep falling from the **magazine** on to my lap.

Master this method and never forget another item at the grocery store.

LET'S BE PRACTICAL -- DAILY CURING

Let's be practical with this memory method. Using it to remember a grocery list is practical, yes, but how else can we use it? How about on a daily basis to remember what we have to do each day. Now that would be practical, wouldn't it?

We all are busy people. Today in particular, though, you have an unusually busy schedule -- lots of errands to run, people to see, things to do. You have to remember to go to the store to get light bulbs and cereal. You want to be sure to stop at the boat show so that you can see that boat that you are always dreaming of owning some day. You have to firm up the airline reservations for your vacation trip. When you get home you have to glue the dish that you broke. And you have to do the income tax report.

Light bulb, cereal, motor boat, airplane, glue, taxes. Six items to remember. You already know that you can remember at least 10 items, and so six items should be a snap.

There is a light bulb eating cereal from a bowl. ZOOM in to the bowl. The cereal is in the shape of motor boats and they are zipping through the milk. One of them zips right out of the bowl into the air and turns into an airplane. The airplane is covered with glue. The airplane flies into a cloud of forms and the forms stick to the airplane. ZOOM into the forms -- they are 1040 Forms, the kind you use for the IRS when you figure your taxes.

Six items on the day's schedule -- none will be forgotten.

EXERCISE

Make a list of 10 items. CURE the items, two at a time. Remember, the more ridiculous the connections, the easier it will be to recall them.

MNEMONICS

Devices that help us to remember are called mnemonics. Do you remember what you were taught in elementary school to help you remember the musical notes on the scale. Chances are good that you remember Every Good Boy Deserves Fun.

The first letter of each word in the sentence represents the notes in the scale: EGBDF.

How about the five Great Lakes? HOMES is the word that comes to mind for me, the word I was taught to connect to the Great Lakes. Each letter is the first letter of one of the lakes: Huron, Ontario, Michigan, Erie, Superior.

Mnemonics need not come in the form of letters or sentences, however. Simply connecting any list to the rooms and areas of your home can be quite effective. For example, if you wanted to remember the order of the first five Presidents of the United States, you might want to connect them in order with the first five rooms or areas they would encounter as they entered your home.

For me, I would visualize Washington in the front hall, Adams in the living room, Jefferson in the dining room, Madison in the family room, and Monroe in the bathroom (with all due respect). Once I have committed the image of each President in his appropriate space, preferably doing something appropriate to the space (e.g. eating dinner in the dining room; watching TV in the family room), I can always remember the order of their presidencies by simply remembering the order of the rooms in my home, something I am not likely ever to forget.

EXERCISE

Take a group of people you normally have difficulty remembering, and create a mnemonic device to help you remember them from now on. Perhaps, for example, you always seem to have difficulty remembering the order of birth of your sister's twelve children: determine the correct order and envision each one in his or her particular space in your home, according to the order of your home. If you do not have 12 rooms, use areas like the front stairs, the patio, the yard, etc. (Don't forget the bathrooms.) Once you have assigned each child a space in the order of your home, according to the order of their birth, you will not forget the order of their birth again.

REMEMBERING STATE CAPITALS

Use the CURE technique to remember the 50 state capitals so that you will never forget. Again, creativity and ridiculousness are in order.

An example of CURING a state to its capital would be New Jersey and Trenton. For me, I simply envision a cow (jersey) in a tent. Tent is enough for me to remember Trenton, but perhaps you would prefer a different connection. (e.g. Ten ton? Train...?)

Another example: I think of a large eye hoeing a field: from nowhere a gang of little boys appears and tramples all that has been hoed. (Idaho: Boise)

Another example: I think of a fur mountain peeling like a banana. Take a minute to imagine it. A mountain made of fur. There it is, sticking up into the sky. All of a sudden, the mountain begins to peel, as if it were a banana. (Vermont: Montpelier)

You get the idea by now, no?

You can CURE countries to their capitals as well, of course.

EXERCISE

Write a list of all 50 states and their capitals. CURE them. (You are much more likely to remember them forever if you CURE them than if I were to provide CURES for you.)

STEP # 3. <u>REMEMBERING NAMES</u>

We forget names because we do not make them stick out in our minds when we hear them. To remember them, we simply have to create a CURE that will trigger them for us.

First of all, get into the habit of **saying the name aloud** as soon as you hear it. This will insure that you insist on hearing it, and that you will ask someone to repeat it if it is mumbled, rather than just letting it go. If you do not hear a name, how can you possibly remember it?

In addition, saying it aloud will give you another sense -- that is, the sense of hearing -- to complement the visual sense that you will use when you create your CURE. When you try to recall the name, you will be able to draw upon how it sounded when you said it.

Ever hear the phrase, connect a name with a face? Well, that is exactly what you need to do to remember names. The name most often should be CURED to the face.

While many names are common, i.e. used often by many different people, faces usually are distinct from person to person. It is likely that you

remember faces, even though you forget names.
Right? That is because 1. You SEE faces and,
when only one sense is being used, it is easier for
most people to remember what is seen as opposed to
what is heard, and 2. While most names are not
distinct, most everyone has some distinct feature in
his or her face -- a high forehead, long sideburns,
big ears, small ears, banana nose, upturned nose,
bushy eyebrows, blonde eyebrows, very long, very
curly hair, very short, very straight hair, etc.

The next time you are introduced to
someone, repeat his name aloud and, as you do so,
note a particular prominent feature on his face. If
there is a prominent feature presenting itself more
readily elsewhere (e.g. a low cut dress), use it, but
know that the more permanent the prominent
feature, the more permanent the memory trigger. If
you rely on a person's clothing or jewelry (e.g. big
earrings), you are not likely to see the trigger the
next time you see the person in another setting. The
face, on the other hand, will remain the same -- same
big ears, or big nose, or bushy eyebrows, or high
forehead, etc.

Use the prominent feature to CURE the
name. For example, you are introduced to Jim. As
you stick out your hand to shake, you say the name
Jim aloud, and you note (without staring) his balding
head. One way to CURE the name Jim to the face

in this instance would be to SEE the name Jim nestled into the bald spot on his head. SEE it as you SAY it. See the letters J-I-M.

SUBSTITUTION ALTERNATIVE

For certain names, like Jim, there is another step you may take. Rather than seeing the name Jim nestled into the bald spot, see a GYM nestled into the bald spot, a real gym, complete with basketball court, parallel bars, hanging rings, wrestling mats, etc. -- whatever YOUR version of a gym looks like.

Do you think that the next time you see Jim, you will also see the GYM nestled in his bald spot? Of course you will. And you will also remember his name.

Jim/Gym is an easy **substitution**, and, though the name itself spelled out in large letters (or small ones, if that works better for you) can work well if it is CURED to a prominent feature of the face, a substitution that is CURED may make the process just a bit easier.

Other examples of substitutions are: Bill/ restaurant bill; Jack/automobile jack; Pat/hand patting; Pete/a patch of peat moss; Mary/marry (picture a bride and groom); John/bathroom (hey, if it works, use it); Peg/wall peg; Carol/caroller (singer); Janet/janitor; etc.

Can you think of ready-made substitutions for names?

EXERCISE

Write down 10 more name substitutions. They do not have to be exact --- the only criterion is that they work for you. For example, if JUICE will help you to remember JOYCE, then it is perfectly fine. (CURE: She has a glass of juice balanced on her curly-haired head.)

IF NO PROMINENT FEATURE...

Not all faces or bodies present a prominent feature so readily. Not a problem. Simply remember that your goal is to make **a connection that is unlikely or ridiculous or extraordinary**.

If Jim does not have a prominent feature, give him one. See him with the gym as a nose. Or simply imagine that he opens his mouth and a series of gyms, dozens of them, come streaming from his mouth. You are not likely to forget that.

The point is to be creative and ridiculous. It is not possible to get stumped for a good CURE as long as you remember that ANY ridiculous connection can work. If you meet Margaret and you cannot think of a substitute for the name Margaret, and she has no prominent feature, just **say** her name aloud and **see** the name Margaret in large letters coming out of her mouth, or sitting on her nose, or sticking out of her ear.

Master this method and you will amaze everyone you meet, especially when you remember their names, and they do not remember yours.

REVIEW

To Remember Names:

1. SAY NAME ALOUD
2. CURE IT (with or without a substitution) TO THE FACE (or other prominent feature)

STEP # 4. <u>REMEMBERING NUMBERS</u>

Have ever forgotten a telephone number? Your social security number? Other numbers?

You should never have to worry about forgetting a number again.

The longest number that the average person must ever remember is either 9 or 10 digits -- a social security number is 9 digits long; a telephone number, with area code, is 10 digits long.

Sure, there are occasions when we may be called on to remember numbers with more digits, but, in fact, 7 digits is most likely the longest number we encounter on a regular basis -- a telephone number in the same area code as ours.

No matter how long the number, the principles to follow are the same.

<u>SIMPLIFY and REDUCE</u>

It makes sense that it is easier to remember 2 or 3 items than 7 or 8 or 9 items, no? That is why you should **simplify and reduce** a telephone number, a social security number, or any other number, to just 2 or 3 items, rather than trying to remember 7 or more individual digits.

   For example, if the telephone number is 593-2478, you would be creating an unnecessary burden for yourself if you tried to remember each individual digit in sequence, such as five, nine, three, two, four, seven, eight.

   It is easier if you think of the first three digits as a number in the **hundreds**, in this case, five hundred ninety-three, said "five-ninety-three." Not only is one three-digit number easier to remember than three individual digits, but it is also easier to visualize, which is important for another step described below.

   In addition, rather than remembering the four remaining digits individually in the balance of the number, reduce them to one number in the **thousands**, to be pronounced in this case "twenty-four seventy-eight" (as opposed to "two thousand four hundred seventy-eight").

   Think and see the four-digit number in the thousands, **but pronounce** it as a series of two-digit numbers.

   In sum, what you are doing in the example above is simplifying the seven-parts of a telephone number into only two parts: that is, one number in the hundreds and one number in the thousands.

The same principle would apply for larger numbers: social security numbers, for example. Take the number 331-28-5796. Simplify and reduce the nine parts into three parts. Remember the number as three-thirty-one, twenty-eight, fifty-seven ninety-six.

EXERCISE

Simplify and reduce the following numbers:

254-8746 (into only two parts)
387-21-9238 (into only three parts)
213-664-2327 (into only three parts)

REPEAT NUMBER ALOUD

It is very important to repeat the number aloud when you are trying to commit it to memory. Again, as in remembering names, SAYING the number will give you a prominent trigger when you try to recall it: you will be able to draw upon how it sounded when you said it.

Saying it only in your mind is not as effective as saying it **aloud**.

GIVE A NUMBER MEANING IF POSSIBLE

Though my college days began three decades ago, I will never forget the post office box number I had at Yale Station in New Haven: 5256.

Did I remember it as five, two, five, six? No. I remembered it as fifty-two fifty-six, and by doing so the number took on additional meaning to me. Though neither History nor Political Science were my favorite subjects, I do remember certain dates very well. One date, for example, is 1066 (ten sixty-six), the year of the Battle of Hastings and the Norman Conquest of England.

I also remember, however, that Eisenhower was elected President of the United States in 1952 and in 1956. The fact that I was alive then, and that I connect other things in my life to those elections and those dates, contribute to my being able to remember those specific years.

Imagine my surprise when I received Box 5256 as my address at Yale. By simply connecting the years of Eisenhower's election victories to my box number, I gave it meaning that will permit me to remember it for the rest of my life.

Of course, it is not always possible to give meaning to a number, but if you can, do so, knowing that it will help you enormously if you wish to remember it.

ENGRAVE OR CHISEL

To help you remember a number, **visualize** it as you say it aloud, and, more important, visualize the number being **engraved into a band of gold**, or **chiseled into a slab of cement**. This visual image, coupled with the auditory clues developed when you say the number aloud, will serve as trigger when you want to recall the number. You want to be able to SEE the engraved or chiseled number and HEAR it pronounced.

If you have a favorite piece of jewelry that can take engraving, ENLARGE the image of the piece of jewelry in your mind and SEE the engraving of the number taking place. By using a piece of jewelry that is familiar to you, you will be giving yourself one more trigger to help visualize the number. Likewise, if you prefer to see the number chiseled rather than engraved, perhaps you can visualize the sidewalk in front of your house, or the base of a statue that has meaning for you. SEE the chiseling taking place. Perhaps it would work better for you if you see yourself taking a stick and engraving it into wet cement. Or perhaps you can visualize yourself or someone else using a jackhammer to etch it into the ground.

Do not feel limited to engraving or chiseling. If carving wood works better for you, use it. Or perhaps a branding iron. Or a paintbrush on canvas. The principle is still the same: SEE the number.

Remember also to SAY the number ALOUD as it is being engraved or chiseled (or carved, etc.).

REVIEW

To Remember A Number:

1. Simplify and Reduce it.
2. Say it Aloud.
3. Give it Meaning, if possible.
4. Engrave or Chisel it into your mind.

STEP # 5. <u>REMEMBERING</u> <u>SPEECHES</u>

More than once, before I began using this system, I delivered an address and left out one or more important points that I had wanted to make. That does not happen to me anymore.

The method is simple. As you review the speech beforehand, list the significant ideas in the sequence in which you will be offering them. The list can be as detailed or as distilled as you wish. In the end, however, you will have a list -- and you already know that you are capable of committing a list to memory, no matter how long.

The worst possible way to deliver a speech is to read it. Unless, of course, your goal is to put the audience to sleep. You must commit your speech to memory, but you need not memorize every single word.

Learn the significant ideas -- as many or as few as you wish. Learn them well, enough so that you can speak with confidence, in your own words, without having to rely on the written speech itself, though knowing that you will always be able to refer to the speech or to notes in the event that you need to or want to.

Now that you know the significant ideas, simply list them. If you can reduce them to single words, great. If not, however, phrases or sentences are fine: whatever works best for you, given the speech's content. Now, just as you would remember a grocery list, or a list of random objects, CURE the speech's significant ideas in pairs.

For example, in a speech I gave once at a dinner to honor the success and achievement of a group of sales people, I broke down the speech into a list of five items to be remembered: 1. humorous opening about the length of the speech, 2. my definition of success, 3. examples of outstanding success, including a quick story about Abraham Lincoln, 4. a brief accounting of how the honorees had succeeded, 5. the impact of the honorees' success on the future of the company.

I simply CURED the elements in pairs.

Humorous opening and definition of success: I envisioned an audience howling in **laughter** (for humorous), and out of their mouths came **dictionaries** (for definitions), actually shooting into the air.

Definition of success and examples: I envisioned the **dictionaries** and **ZOOMED** into the covers, and on the covers were old photos of

Lincoln with just a mustache and no beard, wearing a baseball cap. He looked odd indeed, but that's the point.

Lincoln's success and the honoree's success: Each dictionary, still in the air, with the Lincoln cover, turned into **Lincoln himself**, and now there were dozens of him, and each replica came crashing down with great noise and disruption into the area of tables where the **guests of honor** were seated.

Honorees' success and the future of the company: The **honorees** helped each Lincoln to his feet and removed his baseball cap and replaced it with a space helmet and also offered him sophisticated, futuristic, high-tech gadgets, symbols of the **future**, especially for Lincoln.

My CURES were distilled in my mind as simply:

Laughing audience -- dictionaries shooting from their mouths to the air.

Zoom into a dictionary cover -- it's a photo of Lincoln in a baseball cap.

The dictionaries turn into full replicas of Lincoln himself and

Each Lincoln comes crashing into the tables of the honorees.

The honorees replace the baseball caps with space helmets.

I know: it is crazy, ridiculous, ludicrous. Yes. And that is exactly what I want for my CURES. I remembered the speech without a problem and it went quite well.

Again, if the significant ideas of the speech can be expressed in one or two words, all the better, as long as it works for you. Your speech may have five significant ideas or twenty significant ideas. No matter. Simply CURE the ideas in pairs, and never fear that you will forget.

REVIEW

To Remember Speeches:

1. List the Significant Ideas.
2. CURE Them.

Please address all inquiries on the items below to:
Crimson Blue Publishing, P.O. Box 205, Greenwich,
NY 12834   Telephone: (518) 692-9000

CONSULTING, SPEAKING ENGAGEMENTS, SEMINARS

Inquiries about Dr. Droge's availability and fees for consulting, speaking engagements, or personally conducted seminars.

NEWSLETTER

Inquiries about subscriptions to the quarterly SuperSmart Newsletter, with guides and information to help the reader appreciate success and reach superior levels in various fields.

ADVERTISERS

Inquiries about subsequent editions of this book, which will make limited space available for suitable and appropriate advertisements.

VOLUME DISCOUNTS

Inquiries about the significant discounts available for large volume orders of SuperSmart Systems.

SARATOGA SEMINARS

Inquiries about SuperSmart Systems Seminars, which are available during the year for corporate groups and other large organizations in quaint, historic Saratoga Springs, New York, summer home to the NYC Ballet, the Philadelphia Orchestra, and NY thoroughbred racing.